I REMEMBER GLORIA

I REMEMBER GLORIA

MADONNA KNIGHT

I Remember Gloria
Madonna Knight

Dedicated to my daughters Makeda, Nsenga, Nzinga, Aminah, Nuriddeen, and Faatimah.

Preface

I Remember Gloria is a memoir of events in a brilliant woman's life. In telling the story of my mother I also share the story of my own life, of living with an intelligent, smart but mentally ill and deeply troubled mother.

I hope this story of despair, abuse, adultery, hope, determination, and success will be an inspiration to all —especially the sixteen grandchildren and twenty-four great-grandchildren she left behind.

I Remember Gloria

My mother lived in Guyana, South America where the culture impacted her upbringing and later her marriage. She, like many women, suffered at the hands of their husbands.' Men who felt that loving their wives meant inflicting physical and mental abuse. All of this was passively accepted by the culture. Not a day would pass without hearing about a woman being beaten.

I often wondered how life would have been for my mother if she had been alive for me to consult with and spend quality time with as an adult —as a wife, mother, and grandmother. How she would have loved her grandchildren and traveled the world with them. She would have been proud of the women they've become.

My mother lived on medication for much of her adult life after her divorce from my father. She lived in a culture of subjugation; a society of men who didn't appreciate the role of women in many regards. It was a culture that objectified its women regardless of their education and professional status. Gloria —like many professional women from various parts of the world, left her children and families to study and work abroad. Caribbean women were particularly known to leave the islands looking for job opportunities as nurses and teachers in Europe and America.

Often immigrant women were the main providers for their families. My mom worked several jobs as did many women in her time. They worked hard and often sacrificed their time with their children in the process to make as much money as possible in hopes of purchasing their first home in their new home abroad.

Nurses from the Caribbean were particularly in high demand during the 50s, 60s, and 70s.

During this time it was called the "Brain Drain," which meant that all the well-educated professionals were leaving their countries to seek a better life for their families.

I remember as a little girl hearing conversations by older women, who were all married, saying a few disturbing things like, "If your husband didn't beat you, it meant that he didn't love you". The other was, "Your husband would have several mistresses, that's just the way it is". It was hardly a secret or a surprise if a man fathered several children outside of his marriage. So many children were raised in this type of dysfunction.

I can remember hearing stories of family members' discussions; Did you see so and so's children at his funeral -the ones from the other woman up the street? Other stories would surface about young couples who wanted to get married but couldn't once they discovered they were half-siblings. This would be devastating to the couple because this would also be the first time that the families would meet.

As a child, I was very confused about the notion of women being objectified in any form. Women were expected to work both in the home and outside of the home. Yes, the extended families were available to help when needed but the man's job was never modified in any way.

As I came of age, I could not blindly accept this framework. Women of my era were not different from our mothers regarding our ambitions. Some of us choose to work outside of our homes because we have our ambitions and want to have a career. Sometimes other women worked out of necessity.

During my mother's time, there were no support groups, no shelters, and no counseling for women who had nowhere to go. Women were looked down upon and they felt great shame that they couldn't be honored and respected in the family by keeping their marriage together!

In my generation, there was more support for women educating themselves and women were not confined to staying in a relationship that was unhealthy, abusive, and dysfunctional.

Many children grew up in dysfunctional homes but didn't know it. It all seemed normal because there was no name for it.

Dysfunctional families are not healthy for anyone including the abuser.

As a child I would pray that my parents get a divorce, I just didn't want to hear the arguing and be a witness to my mother being physically abused. In a very strange way, I also began to feel it was normal for a woman to be beaten in a marriage.

The most painful part of some of these episodes was when we witnessed my parents being "lovey-dovey". It just seems like madness, that you would beat a woman —leaving her with black eyes and bruises on her body, and then expect her to be kind, loving, and comforting. I dreamed as a child of my parents fighting to come to an end. For us as children, it was very stressful. We knew that there was "trouble" in our family even though we didn't know to what degree.

The divorce or separation of parents can often be a solution to aiding the children's success in life. Sometimes the adults are so consumed with themselves and their relationships, that the children become a pawn in the middle of the "madness".

The journey through my life has always been an interesting one. As a child, I grew up with two highly educated parents. They were great examples to us in that area of life by always stressing that we should be focused on our education, and in life, we would go "far". We always tried to do our best to get good grades and get into good colleges.

My father had his issues with infidelity. This all started very early in their marriage. I remembered as a little girl constantly being aware of my father's extra-marital affairs.

Unfortunately, the culture "approved" of infidelity. A man could be getting married and sleeping with his mistress at the same time. Both the wife-to-be and the girlfriend knew this. But, the wife-to-be would hope that the infidelity would stop once they got married.

The extended families were aware of the abuse and never got involved. I remember hearing the older women talking amongst themselves saying, "If your man doesn't beat you, it means he doesn't love you." They would say, "The wife has more respect because she is married and he has to take care of her, so she should be happy".

My mother was a beautiful, smart, and intelligent woman who strongly believed in the institution of marriage. She was a devout Christian. Her parents were married for life. We never heard of any abuse from my grandfather towards his wife. She was from a tradition where people stayed married for life. But contrary to my joyful grandparents, I remember as a child seeing my mother dress in her crisp nurse uniform and getting ready for work. She would complete her outfit by wearing a pair of dark shades to cover up her black eye. She would spend hours laying in her bed crying and I never knew why.

As a little girl, I never knew that this was abuse. No one in the family ever came by to comfort her. It all seemed like the norm to us.

Later on in life, through speaking with my relatives, I realized the dysfunction of our family. It did not matter that she was educated and beautiful, she —like too many women, would become a victim and this would be their fate in life.

My parents got the opportunity to go to London, England to work for better wages and to provide a better life for us all. This was very common in the Caribbean, where educated people would leave to live overseas, particularly going to Europe, America, and Canada to provide for their immediate and extended families as well.

They would spend several years in London, England while my grandparents became our caretakers. Grandpa did all the money management and bought all the groceries. My grandmother became blind in her later years. Before she lost her sight completely, she had a business making flowers for people and she sometimes had very rich clients who ordered from her. I recall the velvet material she used. As children, some of us helped. She had a wooden hammer with various shapes, we placed the material on another block of wood and "hammer" the imprint on it. After that, we cut out the shapes and put them on a wire "stick" which she covered with a green velvet ribbon to complete the flowers. Some of us would then be assigned to deliver them to the homes of her clients.

Once she became completely blind, Grandpa took care of her with great pride. My grandparents had seven children.

My parents sent money each month to Grandpa to hire a maid to take care of our needs. Although my grandma was blind, she was so smart. She was able to tell the difference in coins. As children, we would try to trick her into giving us money of higher value. She would give us what she thought was enough money to buy our treats. We were fascinated that she couldn't see us but could know the difference in the value of the coins. We didn't realize that she would feel the edges and face of each coin to know its value. We didn't realize this until we were much older.

My cousin Diana and I had some "fun" games we played. Our home had a tin cover on the roof and when we threw pebbles on it you could hear the rippling sound. Well, we thought that it would be fun to throw it on the side of the house where Grandma slept. She would complain to Grandpa and he would warn us to stop. Grandma would yell out to us "You damn children! —Stop it!". Diana and I would giggle, stay quiet, and pretend it was not us. One faithful day, we tried throwing the pebble on the roof and it went through the window of Grandma's room and landed on her chest. We got scared because that was not our intent. Grandma yelled out "Cecille, these blasted children threw a rock through the window and it landed on my chest". Grandpa hurried into her room to see the commotion. We could hear them talking, he asked her for the rock, and his response was laughable. He said, "Woman, this is a small pebble, relax yourself, the children are having some fun". After this incident, we stopped. Thankfully with all the children in the house, she never knew it was Diane and I messing with her.

I loved combing my grandma's hair while she told us stories about the family. It was a curly thick head of gray hair. Her favorite style was having two thick braids hanging over her shoulders.

Grandpa was a tall strapping man with broad shoulders and a mighty walk and stature. He was stern and intentional about almost everything he did. He was very supportive of his children (all seven of them).

My mom and one of her sisters both became nurses. My other aunt who remained in Guyana died during the delivery of her last child, Ernest. He would be the last of four children.

My Grandpa, was a carpenter by trade, and he made furniture for many households; many of them for many wealthy families. He was also a great cook. For most of our younger years, we enjoyed lots of delicious dishes. One of his favorites was provisions and fish with coconut milk. This is the dish that would make you feel like you could run 2 miles and then fall asleep for an hour. He loved to make another favorite dish for all the children before going to school most mornings. We would all eat plantain porridge mixed with the fresh goat milk we got delivered each day. We were always excited when the milkman came to deliver the milk. Grandpa would warm up the milk in a pot; and when it was cool, I loved sticking my finger in the milk and swirling it at the top of the milk to eat the "skin".

Grandpa was a "man's man", he was gentle and yet stern. He took care of his family and protected them. He treated his wife like a "Queen".

We respected him and admired him, even more so as an adult now as I reflect on him.

There were times I would get up each morning and get on his bike to go to the

"Bourda Market"(this is an open Farmers Market) to buy fresh fish and vegetables from the vendors.

He would place me on the handlebar of the bike and off we went shopping. He would hold my hand while holding his basket in the other as he bartered with each vendor. He never paid full price for anything! I watched him barter with each vendor for fish, provisions, and vegetables. We hardly ate meat; most of our food was prepared with provisions, vegetables, and seafood. We would eat poultry on holidays like Christmas and New Year's.

Our heaviest meal was around 1 pm. In the evening we had tea, cheese, and crackers before we went to bed. This was one of our social times to talk as a group/ family.

There were two girls and six boys in our home. My brothers; Donald, Victor, and Peter, Diana —my older cousin; and her brothers; Leslie, Melvin, and Ernest. My mother sent money to hire a maid to prepare our meals and a seamstress to make our uniforms, and regular clothing. My parents built a two-story home with three large rooms, a living room, a dining room, and a kitchen. The boys had their room and Diana and I had ours. Grandma and Grandpa had theirs; however, my grandfather slept in a rocking chair he placed in front of the girls' room to make sure we didn't sneak out to meet our friends at night.

My cousin was older than I was and she loved to party as a teen; she would wait until my "Grampey" fell asleep and sneak out to run up the street and party. I was her "cover' and "lookout" to see if our grandpa would be coming up the street on his bike.

She would always be getting into trouble for sneaking out and she and Grandpa would get into it! I remember a time when she was not allowed to go to a party and she snuck out of the house. While dancing with her boyfriend, I was placed on the steps to see if Grandpa was looking for us. Well, this was our unlucky night. Some of her friends saw him approaching the house and announced his arrival. She grabbed me and ran down the street laughing while my heart was pounding out of my chest. I knew what was in store for us. Grandpa always took off his big leather belt, and that was for whooping our butts. He would often threaten us and not go through with the threat. When we got home, we crawled under our big queen size bed.

This bed was high off the floor and it was big enough to sit under. My cousin decided to get a one-burner gasoline stove. She would get a pot and all the food she wanted to cook. We made an entire meal in that room while she told stories and I listened. She was an excellent cook and still is!

Life was beautiful growing up in Guyana! We often traveled to Mackenzie from Georgetown to visit my father's parents. It was nice going there, especially because they had lots of fruit trees like sour cherries, soursop, mangoes, stink toe, guava, bananas, five fingers, and more. My favorites were sour cherries and sour mangoes. I would sometimes hide under the bed and eat my cherries and sour mangoes until I got caught.

Children rarely got sick because of all the fruits they eat; we truly believe it was from the high concentration of vitamin C.

My parents would later migrate to the United States. They left us with our grandparents for several years. I don't believe it was because they wanted to. But like many parents traveling to America for a 'better' life, they could not afford to take the entire family at the same time.

Many couples in the Caribbean often left their children behind in the care of their relatives until they were able to afford to send for them.

My brothers and I were "sent for" at the ripe age of thirteen, ten, eight, and six. When we heard we were going to America, of course, we were happy; we heard wonderful stories about America. One famous story was always told by relatives who lived in America; they always mentioned that the streets were "paved with gold" and you could get rich. So lots of people were happy to have that opportunity to travel overseas. As children, we truly believed the streets were paved with gold.

When the time came we were happy to finally travel to live with our parents. We were excited! What we remembered of them was that twice a year we would receive several barrels of clothes and toys from America — those were exciting times for us as children.

My grandmother would start singing a song by the Beatles. It was "I am leaving on a jet plane, I don't know when I'll be back again". She always loved us. She was a kind and generous woman. A woman of mixed race (Portuguese and African) ancestry. Beautiful to look at, and medium in height. My cousin and I would often comb her hair and clean up her room. There were only two girls in the house with six boys, yet we were expected to do most of the chores, which was our tradition.

My mother came home several times a year to visit, and I recall one night seeing my mother in the living room with my grandfather. He was sitting as he usually did in his rocking chair. My mother was sitting on the floor with her head in his lap crying. My grandfather held her and tried to comfort her sadness as he stroked her hair.

She was very close to her parents and she made sure that she took care of them. When my parents went back to America, that's when my mother hired an additional housekeeper to make our clothes and take care of the chores around the house. My mother felt it was too much for my grandfather to take care of eight children and a blind wife; even though he volunteered and loved taking care of us. No longer did my cousins and I have to do chores or cook. Everything was done for us.

My parents worked hard in America and send money back to take care of all of our needs. Because of them we were able to live a comfortable upper middle class life in Guyana.

I loved being a child growing up in Guyana before my teen years. There were trees to climb, dogs to chase, and bathing in the ocean when we wanted. Picking a variety of fruits and just having fun.

Driving in the "jungle" in the back of an open truck we would laugh and scream as we held onto the truck as the adults laughed at us. There are coconut trees to attempt to climb and often slide down for lack of expertise. Some boys climbed the very tall trees as if they were walking up the tree. We often sat on the ground and looked to the sky as they threw the coconut down to us and we dodged getting hit on the head. I loved climbing the 'five-finger" tree and eating its fruits with a bit of salt. It was a sweet and sour fruit that made me happy every time I ate it.

When my mother came to visit she would wake us up at sunrise and dress us in sweaters for the early morning cool breeze. We would put on our slippers and begin walking up and down Hatfield Street towards the 'Sea Wall' while holding hands, singing, laughing, and playing until we got to the bleachers.

We would sit on the bleachers, and that's where the fun would begin. The water would clash against the walls as the ocean breeze chased the water towards us. We screamed and laughed as we got soaked. My mom would then point to the sun rising as the beautiful rainbows presented themselves; as we looked in amazement at how perfectly the colors were. As the water receded, we would then jump off the bleachers and "chase" the waves as they revealed dozens of crabs crawling on the sand. All the children would begin to chase the crabs as they ran back into their holes in the wet sand. My mom would laugh at us as she walked along the shores behind us. The ocean breeze felt so good in the early mornings.

It was 1971 when my grandparents received our plane tickets to America. It was a joyous and sad time in my life. I would be leaving my cousin who was like my big sister, my other cousins who were like brothers, and my grandfather who took care of us for several years. My grandmother; whose hair I would miss combing and helping to bring her meals. My brothers would be leaving their male cousins that they played with endlessly.

We would be leaving lots of yard space where we played into the night. Unafraid of anything because we were always safe. Neighbors were always looking out for all the children. So as the adults hung out on the porch at night talking and catching up the children would play.

I would miss getting up at early dawn with the hens making their signature sound at sunrise. There was no clock to wake us up; the hens were our alarm clock. I'd miss going to school in my crisp brown pleated uniform and tie around my crisp white-collar neckline. Being taught by the nuns and having my nails inspected each morning to see if there was any dirt; when we got to school, we would have to line up in a straight line to have our uniform inspected. If your nails were not clean and the uniform was not pressed, you would get tapped with a ruler in front of the entire class. This was considered to be an embarrassment!

After school, many children loved to go across the street to the largest Catholic Church (Brickdam) in Guyana. We lived across from our school and Church. It was our special triangle. We lay on the grass for what would seem like hours before we went home.

We lay there talking about traveling to distant places like London and New York. Many of us knew we were leaving and it was bittersweet with our friends. Someone would quickly change the topic and start to play and we would try to catch grasshoppers as we put them in bottles. We kept them in bottles and punch holes in the metal covers for air. We check every day to see if their transformation from caterpillars into beautiful butterflies took place. We would then let them go free, as we watch them fly into the sky.

Playing in the rain with no care for being soaked or getting a cold was not a thought! It was total fun, freedom, and being a child. Parents never fussed because they'd join the fun themselves. We would soon be dry as the sun beamed on us after it rained for about ten to fifteen minutes as we walked home. It was one of those fun things we did very often. There would be so much we would soon realize that would not be the same. Our lives would soon change drastically.

The day of our departure to America soon came. My brothers and I would be traveling alone and in the care of an airline stewardess. This would be the first time that we traveled alone without an adult; when we arrived at the airport we were escorted by a stewardess, who we were told would be responsible for us and we should listen to her. It was a bit stressful because this was all new to us. I asked to sit next to the window because I wanted to see the sky which I often looked up to as a child. Now it was me who would be traveling through the sky. The sky was a mystery, a place that I thought other people lived in, but as we traveled through the sky, I soon realized no one lived there and there were layers of clouds. It was scary and fascinating all wrapped up in one.

I was awake throughout the trip. We traveled on PAN AM Airlines. It was strange to sit for that many hours.

We arrived in America at night. I remember seeing from the sky as we were approaching landing what seemed to be an ocean of flickering lights. It was amazing and exciting at the same time. I remembered the anticipation of what all the lights might mean.

The stewardess approached us and escorted us to our parents; who were waiting with the other parents who were waiting for their children to come to America. I was so excited to see the golden streets that my older relatives talked about.

We arrived at our home in Brooklyn on Dean Street during the night; so I couldn't tell what my surroundings looked like. I knew something was different, but I couldn't wait to see my room. To my surprise, I would be sharing a room with my brothers.

In Guyana, I shared a large room with my other female cousin while my brothers and my male cousins shared a room.

The following morning I wanted to go outside and was told, "You can't go outside as you did in Guyana, it's different in America," this confused me for a while until I realized that my parents were renting the top floor of the house we lived in. We weren't free to play, run, jump, and do all the things we were accustomed to as children.

Our lives were now confined to the space my parents rented. We spent a lot of our free time watching Black and White television for hours. This was something we never had growing up in Guyana. My grandfather didn't want one. He felt that children should be out playing and being creative with their time. My uncle owned a bar and we stopped by once in a while to watch TV when we visited.

We started school several months after we arrived and realized that even school was different. Students were rude to their teachers. They were talking back to the authority figures in the school while the teachers were giving instructions. There seemed to be no consequences for their behavior.

This was unlike what we were accustomed to in our schools. Children were "seen and not heard" during school. They had to respect the teachers and all authority figures. We only answered questions when asked. If we did make a mistake and disrespect the teachers, we would be disciplined by both our teachers and the Headmaster (Principal); then when we got home our parents laid it on us as well.

Being a teacher was one of the most honorable positions there was in my country. Your parents and elders came first and then your teachers.

I was twelve and confused with my new culture. In the sixth grade, I was introduced to cigarettes in the girl's bathroom. Girls were hanging out sharing cigarettes and smoking. They would "cut" classes sometimes all day in the bathroom. It was crazy to me!

One day after resisting many temptations and the pressure of my peers encouraging me to smoke, I gave in. I took my first "puff" and began coughing nonstop while the girls stood around laughing. After that experience, I realized that this activity was not something I wanted to be involved in. That day I went home and told my older cousin Leslie -who also lived with us and smoked, he was an adult and would smoke when my parents were not home. He advised me not to tell my parents because I would get into serious trouble.

Family life was decent. My parents would take us out every other weekend for Chinese food. It was something to look forward to on top of our tradition of having breakfast and dinner together regularly. Soon we would be filled with exciting news of moving to our new home. I would finally get my room, as I had back in Guyana. We would be free to run and play in our backyard. We would enjoy ourselves as children again. But this joy would soon change to drama and heartbreak.

After moving to America our parents' marriage seemed fine to us as children for a while. Only a few years after moving into our new home, they filed for divorce. A word I had never heard of, this too had to be explained to us. What did this mean? As we'd come to learn, our lives would not be the same way we once thought itwould be.

I began to notice my mother on many occasions in the mornings getting ready for work in her nurse's uniform and completing it with a pair of dark shades. It brought back my childhood memories of the fighting in Guyana.

My mother was still being abused but in silence. There was no loud crying or loud outburst. All I saw was my mother on many mornings leaving the house with dark shades on. I didn't realize at the time what was going on, but as time went by I began to figure it out.

My father's indiscretions of multiple affairs also began to take its toll on our mother.

As life began to play with my head, I began to remember in Guyana when my parents got into many fights. I never realized as a child what the word for it was. It seemed to be 'normal' to my siblings and me. The women around us would always talk about being 'hit' by their husbands — they would repeatedly say that "if your husband did not hit you it meant that he did not love you."

It was common knowledge when a husband 'beat' his wife. Back in Guyana I recall, my mother had gone to welcome my father home from the military. She was greeted by one of his mistresses who was pregnant with his child while my mother was also pregnant with my brother. I remember her grabbing my hands very tight while the "other" woman slapped her in the face. My mom didn't hit her back. She just stood there as the tears rolled down her face.

She finally spotted my father and called out to him. He grabbed my mother and put us in a car, sending us home.

As we drove off, I turned and saw him grabbing the other woman. My mother kept her head straight, not looking around.

My mother got home and put me to bed then she went to bed herself. I recall her crying softly in the dark. He arrived home hours later.

As soon as he got home he began putting away all the knives.

They began arguing and it became loud. Then it got physical until the fight came into the room where my brothers and I shared a bunk bed. I slept on the top bed. I remembered my father leaning up on the bed and as I screamed leaning over the bed with a bottle in my hands.

Just as I was about to hit him on the head, my older cousin came in at the same time and grabbed me off the bed, and took me out of the house and across the yard to my grandparent's home.

Over time my father's indiscretions contributed to my mother's mental breakdowns. She had first gone into the hospital for a short weekend stay. As kids, we were simply told that she was not feeling well. There were times when the police were called to our home but they never arrested my father even though she had visible bruises on her face and arms.

It was common knowledge that when officers came to the home of an abuser, they would tell the man to calm down and go for a walk; while leaving the wife in distress.

It often seemed as though the officers thought women must have caused their abuse. As children, this pattern of abuse became our norm and like many women of that time, I think my mother assumed she would just have to live with it. As kids, we were also upset at our mother for calling the police on our father.

My father in many ways was a product of his culture, starting in his country and continuing through the 70s when they were married. His was a culture that disregarded women's dignity, respect, and humanity. Women back then and even now in some places in the world are nothing more than objects. They are only valued when their husbands value them.

Sometimes women also see themselves as objects. Imagining their only purpose in life is to care for their husbands while disregarding themselves.

My mom had her first of many mental breakdowns when I was in high school. She was hospitalized for what we were told was a "female problem". We never realized how serious this illness would become and how it would affect us.

My father moved out and moved in with one of his mistresses leaving us with our mother. She was distraught over the separation even though there were good reasons for the marriage to end.

I was fifteen at the time, quiet yet bold with my thoughts toward my mother. I was angry at her for not being strong, for not being healthy. I was angry she would come to my school dressed inappropriately, during her manic episodes she would wear lots of flowers in her Afro and walk the streets barefoot.

She would come to my high school asking for me. This was a big high school and I was not known by most of the students. So I thought I was safe from the embarrassment of a "crazy" mother.

During these times my mother would spend days and nights not sleeping. She'd stay up all night burning candles throughout the house -we were always afraid that the house would one day burn down with us in it.

My brothers and I sometimes did not get any sleep because of this. At times she'd read her bible all day and into the night. Other times she would stand by the street corners and read Bible scriptures. I still thought that if she wanted to "snap out" of this craziness, she really could do it.

There were times she came to my school and a few close friends would inform me. The other kids would laugh at her —and I would too, from a distance. There were several exits at my school; I went to Erasmus Hall High School in Flatbush, Brooklyn. I would leave from an exit far from her and walk home quickly.

Once she stopped working, we realized that she was seriously ill. Her mental breakdowns began to happen more frequently. We had food to eat and some neighbors would look out for us because they knew what was happening to her.

My attitude towards my mother began to change during the 11th grade. At this time my parents had divorced and we moved to an apartment with my mother. I wondered why we were not able to stay in the house we lived in that our parents bought.

My brothers were coming of age and I became the primary caretaker of them and my mother.

None of my friends knew what I was dealing with. They only knew of some surface things. I made sure of this when I went to school. Every school day I went off to classes while my mother slept due to the medication she was taking. She was deteriorating fast but sometimes she was still able to get a part-time job and pay the bills.

The first time my mother ever disappeared and did not come home for several weeks was when I was in my first year of college at Hunter University in New York. She said that she was going to visit a friend in Philadelphia. I didn't know where she was in Philadelphia and I didn't care.

It meant we would have some sanity while she was gone. It meant that we could sleep through the night without worrying if the house would burn down with us in it. It meant not seeing her on the streets walking barefoot and being embarrassed. She left and didn't return for several weeks. However, by the sixth week, I began to worry because we were running out of food and the bills were coming in.

I turned to the superintendent of the building we lived in. She lived across the hall from us and knew the situation we were in.

The superintendent had two sons who were the same age as my younger brothers and they played together and became good friends. Sometimes she would feed my brothers when I had late classes. She encouraged me to continue going to school, she became my "surrogate mother". I depended on her to "look out" for my brothers. She and her husband were from Georgia, Down South. One of her favorite things to do was eat cornstarch from the box. I thought that was so strange. In my culture, we used corn starch for stiffening our cloth. However, that was her thing! She said she was iron deficient, and that women Down South eat cornstarch. When the boys came home from school, she would perch herself on the window and watch her sons and my brothers play until it was time to come in for dinner.

Our superintendent was such a blessing in our lives at such tender ages.

Several weeks passed and my mother had not returned. This was a big change for us. Now we had no money and our food supply was running low. I was confined to one meal a day and the super advised me to go and apply for public assistance. I didn't know what it was other than hearing about it on the news.

We came from an upper-middle-class family raised by our loving grandparents in Guyana, became a working-class two-parent family filled with the turmoil of domestic abuse, and later a broken family with my mother struggling with her sanity. Now we were abandoned and struggling to get even our basic needs met.

I was in college and had some experience traveling and finding my way around

Brooklyn and some parts of Manhattan. Still, I hesitated in hopes that my mother would return soon; she didn't return and I had no choice but to go to the welfare office.

So I did, I took myself to the welfare office in downtown Brooklyn and pretended that I was older than I was. I lied and told them that my father was nowhere to be found. I told them my mother had left and I didn't know where she was. That she was mentally ill and often left, however, this was the longest she had gone. She had never left for more than two days. Now, it seemed that she was not returning.

I was not asked to produce any documents other than a letter from the super stating that we were "abandoned" by our mother and father. I told them we needed money for rent and food. My superintendent never told the landlord what was going on with us. I was a shy young woman and didn't express myself much, I would just do what needed to be done and I was determined. I never tried to call my father and we didn't know where he lived.

To me, he was non-existent in our lives. He rarely showed up to see us while we were living with our mother.

I often thought of the many ways I could have gone astray as a young woman. There were so many opportunities to be promiscuous, hang out with boys, party, and use drugs to escape. But, I always asked God for help and guidance to lead us to the right path and protect us.

There were so many times I wanted to go out partying or just hang out with friends and be a young person with not much care in the world.

After several weeks, my mom came home. She was in the hospital asylum in Philadelphia. She was picked up for claiming that she was President Carter's wife.

At the time I didn't know that she was writing lots of letters to the White House. The next time she went missing she was in Washington, DC. I became seriously concerned about her safety.

She had gone to the White House several times before.

One day, three white men showed up at our apartment looking for my mother. When I answered the door, there were three men in black suits with white shirts, black ties, and shiny black shoes. You could see your face in them. They asked if they could come in to talk with me.

The conversation began with asking me if I knew where my mother was. I told them that she often left and this was the longest she'd been gone. They asked if they could check her room. When they entered the room there were lots of candles and letters on her dresser and bed. I never entered my mother's bedroom when she was not there.

They didn't stay long, they just told me she was in the hospital in Washington, D.C., and would be released soon. They wished us "good luck" and left with some of the letters.

Mom and me

*Me as a child in
my church clothes*

Mom in her younger years

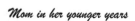

Mom in her nurse uniform

My "high-school sweetheart" and I.

Yusuf and one of our daughters

I was now nineteen years old and completely responsible for my younger brothers.

When she came back home it seemed that she could not remember any of the events she had experienced or was involved in. She continued to have longer spells of mental breakdowns and longer stays in the hospital. I never went to visit her there because somewhere in the back of my mind I still believed she could "snap out of it" if she wanted to.

It was not until I studied Psychology in college that I began to understand a bit about what my mother was experiencing. It was because of my mother that I decided to major in psychology, I wanted to know what was going on with her. I wanted to help "fix it," whatever the "it" was. I wanted to figure out why she couldn't move on and start a new life.

As I attended classes, I "burned" to figure all of it out. The life we had in Guyana with our grandparents, friends, and family was the happiest we had been as young children. We had support and love.

I burned the midnight oil to study and was intense about getting good grades. I dug into studying the human mind and why some people have these experiences, why others seem to be "stronger" with handling these life crises; why some of us are stuck in the past; why some people move on with their lives and seem to be functioning. There were so many whys!

I began to come to terms with the reality that my mother was truly suffering from a legitimate illness. I gravitated to studying psychology because I wanted to know what was going on with my mother and I soon realized that she had lost a piece of herself that she had no control over.

The years of being raised as a young girl and being told that her role in life was to get married, have babies, be submissive, tolerate disrespect, be shamed in public, tolerate infidelity and abuse no matter what because "at least you are married" convinced her that these things were ok.

My studies of psychology would open my eyes to the world of mental illness. I realized that my mother's illness was not a joke. It was not something to be embarrassed about. She couldn't get well on her own; my wishing and hoping were just that. It was a serious mental disorder, aided by the abuse and heartbreak she suffered while married. It was a lot for me to grapple with.

It was in my second year in college that I decided to visit my mother in the asylum at Kings County Hospital. I had gone before to take her food but never stayed. I would give the nurses the food and never tell them who I was.

I decided to visit my mother another time and be brave about what I was about to witness in a mental institution. As I approached the ward where my mother was kept, I could feel my heart coming through my chest. My head was pounding and a voice was telling me to "turn around and leave, -no one will know that you came and no one would care". The smell of the place was unbearable for me. I pushed forward and approached the nurses at the front desk and asked for Gloria.

They asked who I was and I told them I was her daughter. They all looked at me in dismay and responded that they did not think she had any family. I cracked a small smile because I knew that if they knew what I had gone through they would understand —or maybe not, why it took me this long to get the courage to visit. I never told my brothers because I still wanted to protect them from it all.

As I walked through the halls toward my mother's room. I witnessed people strapped to their chairs and people whose arms were stuck to their sides, talking to themselves. There was fear, terror, and sometimes violence in their eyes. They were strapped for fear that they might hurt themselves or others in the ward. I was scared as I walked slowly down the hallways toward her room.

As I walked through the halls, I heard various patients speaking incomprehensible gibberish. The smell was so nauseating and upsetting! I wondered why she was in this type of environment.

As I opened the door she was sitting by the window looking outside. I called out to her but she didn't respond. I realized at that moment how serious my mother's mental illness had become.

The nurse approached her and informed her that her daughter was there to visit her. As she turned, I stood in silence and stared while tears rolled down my cheeks. No words were exchanged. I just stood there! My mind kept flashing back and forth to a simpler happier life in Guyana. Why had this happened to her?

This could not be real, I was not here; please help me, God! She didn't say a word. The nurse held me and said it would be O.K. I cried like a baby in serious pain.

The pain all over my body was intense. The nurse was also from Guyana, she continued to hold me until I calmed down. My mother didn't say a word and I started to imagine what her thoughts were; did she recognize me? Why was she not speaking? The nurse said she had just received her medication and sometimes it takes a few minutes for her to be alert.

This was not the mother who was an artist. A brilliant woman who; despite her early onset of mental illness was able to become a Supervising Nurse. How could this person be the daughter who helped, loved, and took care of her parents and supported her siblings now be alone and lonely with no one to care for her?

Years before, my mother had painted a portrait of herself as a young woman that her parents took great pride in, they hung it up in their home for many years. It was a perfect image of herself that no one could believe she painted it.

My mother was a brilliant woman and I could not believe that she was now in a room looking out of a window with no one to care for her. In a room the size of a closet; a room that seemed like a prison to me; a room with no life present; and a place where no one would come to rest and get well!

Most of her siblings were in London and those that were in America didn't show up for her. Yet she helped many of them to travel overseas to be educated.

As I sat in the room with my mother, she stared at me and I stared back at her. Her stare was that of a daze. It did not seem like she recognized me. The nurse told me that she spent most of her time sitting by the window, staring. They told me that she spoke of her children but they did not know if her thoughts were imaginary or real.

I believed that the nurses treated her with special care because she was also a nurse and many of them could relate to the culture of abuse. I stayed for a short time because she was non-responsive.

As I left the ward where my mother stayed, the nurses asked me to come back more often. I nodded my head and walked through the doors. As I walked it seemed as if I was moving in slow motion. I couldn't wait to breathe some fresh air, to see the trees and flowers. As I walked back home, a short distance from the hospital, it seemed far — ten blocks away from the hospital was longer than usual. I was in a daze and yet happy that I dared to visit my mother.

I realized this was a different world than I was accustomed to. I believed that I was in a trance for a few days after leaving my mother in the mental ward. I could still smell the odor of the hallways, and the images of both young and older people strapped down with their arms tied to their sides.

I couldn't help but wonder what would become of them.

This would slowly become a habitual journey for me, visiting the asylum to visit my mom whenever I could. In a way it served its purpose to keep me distracted from the woes of teenage life while I was involved with taking care of my younger brothers and being concerned with my mother.

Our father was not around regularly. He was off living his life without a care for her and us. When he felt an obligation to check on us he would stop by the apartment to check on my brothers.

I began to develop a deep resentment toward him. I didn't speak to him when he came around.

My mother would eventually come home and I was more aware of what to observe about her illness. I was now responsible for her taking her medication regularly. There were times she would not take her medication and I would begin to see the signs. The ritual would begin with her not sleeping and her eyes would become glossy.

The spirit in her face would become distant and she would be withdrawn. She began reading her bible and started burning more candles. I would question her about taking her meds. She would sometimes not tell the truth and I would get upset with her. We decided to go to her appointments together. This was very helpful in understanding what she needed to keep her "normal" and have a "life".

Several years had passed. My father took my brothers to live with him as they became teenagers. My oldest brother Donald joined the Marines. My younger brothers' Victor and Peter spent the rest of their teen years with my father. I stayed with my mother to assist her.

During those years there were some happy moments and unsettling times in my life. My brothers grew up without any other dramatic events in their lives as young men. It was not easy navigating my life as a teenager/young adult and a caretaker of both my brothers and my mother.

As life would happen, I met my future husband in the 12th grade. We happened to sit next to each other and became good friends. We became high school sweethearts; spending a lot of time together practically every day of the week except the weekends. He walked me home every day and became friendly with my brothers and mother. He was very fond of my mother and enjoyed talking with her.

At that time I never thought he'd become my husband. He was just my boyfriend; someone to distract me from the stresses of all the responsibilities I had. Our time together would be short because his parents "sent for him" to return to Trinidad and Tobago. We continued to write letters each week. We both looked forward to hearing from each other. It was too expensive to call. I believe we may have talked on the phone once in the two years he was away. I continued with my studies. I never told him what I had gone through with my mother. When he met her she seemed "normal".

I kept every letter he wrote in a special flower box on my dresser. The times I felt lonely I read those letters to fall asleep; in hopes that he would return to rescue me. He always told me that when he first saw me he knew that I would be his wife. It was interesting because I was the one who had great insight into my life and sometimes others. He would always call and ask me about the clothing he was wearing when we were in high school, and I got it right most of the time.

He was fascinated with my ability to have such insight. There were times when he asked too much and I decided to stop telling him. I laughed at him because no one knows how the future would turn out.

I knew that he was a kind soul and I wanted to be with him.

He went back to Trinidad only one year into our relationship. He was there because he had to get his green card fixed and he was no longer allowed to stay in America.

He was gone for two years and I continued my college education. I never revealed to him that my mother was mentally ill during our time together. I didn't date anyone else, I was focused on finishing school and helping to supervise my mother and younger brothers.

During those two years, life changed drastically again.

At some point during college I went to live with my father because my mother and I were not getting along. She now had some mental stability and went back to work. She blamed me for her getting a divorce from my father. She would often say, "If it was not for you I would still be married even if your father beat and cheated on me. Now I have nothing."

I would listen and sometimes not respond. However, the times I did respond, I made remarks to her that were hurtful. I often told her that I would rather spend time in jail than have any man or anyone abuse me. They don't own me and I would rather kill them than be abused like that". She would remain quiet as I lashed out at her. I often said to her that she was stupid for staying in a marriage where her husband did not respect and value her. "You are staying in a marriage because you are afraid of being alone". "You are staying in a marriage because of your religion". "You are staying in a marriage because you want to say that you are married; what is wrong with you".

I never told her of the times my father brought his girlfriends to the house when they had parties as many Caribbean people did during the 1970s in Brooklyn. He would have parties and ask one of his friends to cover for him by saying the woman was with them.;

But I know she suspected those women who came to the house without a partner may well be his girlfriend.

I knew who they were because those were the same women whose homes he'd stay in, eat, and make himself very comfortable.

I remember recognizing a few of them because he took me to their homes, sometimes pretending that he was stopping by a friend's house to pick up something. I remember the visit as long as he left me with the woman's child while he entered the bedroom for a while.

I was always told to keep a secret for him because my mother would be upset if she knew. So, I kept the "secret" for a while. I was such an angry young woman who wanted my life to be normal.

One of these women would be the one he moved in with after my parents' divorce. I had no other place to live and so I moved in with them when my mother and I could not get along. He never married the mistress and I was not clear if the child she had was his and didn't ask or care, I resented her as well.

I went along with their rules for as long as I could.

One day I was sitting outside my father's house with some of my friends on the block and saw a woman in the distance walking down the streets towards the house. My heart sank because I knew that we were discovered. My mother didn't know for months where we were and I never told her when I moved out. I quickly called my brothers into the house and locked the door. No one knew that she was our mother because everyone on the block thought that my father's girlfriend was our mother.

She approached the house and began to call our names. She demanded that we come out of the house and speak to her. We kept quiet as I peeked through the curtains at her. She stayed for what seemed like hours. My father was not home.

I realized that she was not on her medication and her attire resembled what she'd worn when she was ill. My father came home after work and saw her sitting on the steps and they began to argue. He called the police to have her removed. She left and stayed at the corner for some time. My father decided he would take us to the Chinese restaurant which was something we did on the weekend.

My mom noticed that we were leaving and approached the car blocking him from leaving. She started banging on the hood of the car and he started to edge up as if he would drive over her. He stopped the car and got out and approached her. He tried pushing her away as we sat watching her crying and calling our names.

He was able to get back in the car but before he could drive off, she held onto the car door as he tried to drive off, she would not let go. He picked up speed and she fell to the ground crying, "Why are you doing this to me." I sat in shock as tears began to roll down my cheeks in silence. I turned around and saw her on the ground. At that moment I wished she would die because I wanted us to be normal. I wanted her to go away. I wanted to be at peace.

We all sat in silence in the car as we went to the restaurant.

I couldn't eat anything once we arrived at the restaurant. I stayed quiet as I was asked what was wrong with me because I knew in reality that I was just a "child" who no one wanted to hear from. As life would move me, every part of my being and consciousness would continue to hurt.

She would continue to come back to the house for several weeks after. Eventually, my father and his girlfriend bought a house in Queens, NY where we all moved to.

My acceptance of the mistress was something I wanted to be comfortable with. But eventually, we started to argue. I could not stand that she was a part of dissolving our family.

I was so enraged that I did not speak to my father that entire evening. My father seemed to dismiss the event that we had just experienced. I made a decision that night in my heart that I was going back to live with my mother. I could not bear the thought that she would not see any of her children.

I was old enough to make my own decisions. I was in college now and I knew this was wrong for her to be treated the way he had treated her. I wanted to live a happy life. I wanted to finally feel like a teenager, a young adult without all this burden of the "crazy" lady who came to the block calling us but she was my mother, so I decided I had to do my best to help take care of her. I felt my heart broken even more when I saw her on the ground. This was not a "crazy" woman, this was my mother, the woman who loved me unconditionally and I knew that I owed her all that I could give. I was becoming a woman and knew I would never wanted to be treated the way we were treating her that day.

Not long after I moved back to Brooklyn to live with mother.

Once I left my father's house, I did not look back and did not care about him. I was now a woman who needed to protect my sanity and my soul.

This was not "alright" with me anymore. I began to feel upset at myself. I never felt the treatment she received from him was ok. For me not being able to do more as a daughter. I felt somewhat responsible for some of it. My brothers grew up in my shadow. We never discussed our mother's abuse. We talked about her "condition" but never discussed the abuse.

One day I got the courage to talk to my mother about her mental illness. At this point, she was having a fairly normal life once again, staying on her medication regularly and not having any more mental breakdowns.

I was coming-of-age as a young woman and I asked her why she didn't divorce my father much sooner. Her answer confirmed my observation as a little girl. As a teenager and now a young woman who was beginning to consider marriage.

She said something so profound that her answer will be forever imprinted in my memory. She said, "I stayed because when you get married, you should stay married for life. It's an honor to be married, especially for a woman. It gives a woman a certain status in life that someone wants to marry her. Even if you were getting beaten at least you were married".

I listened with great trepidation and thought to myself, how come such an intelligent and smart woman could subject herself to this type of ordeal?

She also reminded me that she got a divorce because I always said to her "You should divorce him because you don't deserve this" She said I used to say this to her often. So she did and now she has to deal with it.

My mother returned to her job once again and became a supervising nurse despite her illness. I made sure she took her medication and tried to build a relationship with her.

A relationship with my mother was very important to me. It was also important to my brothers.

After observing my parent's marriage and my mother's mental illness; I made some very conscious decisions about my future relationships. I decided that no one would be allowed to abuse me in any form. That no woman should be disrespected and humiliated like my mother. Yet, I knew in my heart that a woman was being abused every day. However, I can only control what I allow myself to accept.

My mother decided to live on her own. She had her apartment. My brothers would visit often and we had some good times. She started to date from time to time —I was very protective of her.

I was now more than halfway through college and decided to get married to my high school sweetheart.

He had finally returned from Trinidad. I never revealed to him that my mother was ill and so he didn't know all the trials I'd been through with her while he was away. He met her when she was doing better so I thought it was better not to tell him about my secret.

We got married in my third year of college. As we started our own family my mother started to have several relapses. Now I had to reveal to my husband 'my big secret'.

Several times she came by our home and broke the windows, and then proceeded to read the bible.

At this juncture, both my husband and I accepted Islam. When we became Muslim our lifestyle changed drastically. Our social life was different; including our diet and behavior. My husband had already accepted Islam in Trinidad and I waited for him to return to America and then I took my shahada (acceptance of Islam and belief in one God). I have always worked towards being a spiritual person and wanted more structure in my life. I wanted my children to be raised in a home with respect, pride, belief, commitment, spirituality; and the belief in one God.

My husband was very supportive and loved my mother as a person. He was very sympathetic and encouraged me to get her help.

As I became a woman and then a mother, I realized how much I didn't understand as a child what mental illness was.

Unfortunately, while my empathy for my mother grew, my dislike of my father continued to grow stronger. I disliked his type of "manhood" and decided to stop speaking to my father for over fifteen years. I erased him from my life. He was not discussed at all. The only time I heard of him was when my brothers spoke of some conversation they had.

I began to feel the loss of my mother's love and relationship, especially when I began to have my children.

My mother only met three of her six granddaughters. She loved them and I tried to have a better mother/daughter relationship with her. I never realized how that relationship would affect me in life. I suffered in silence as I am sure my brothers did too.

I began to work as a counselor after graduating from college; my commitment was to help young women to improve their self-esteem and consciousness regarding themselves so that they will always matter first. That "we" as young and adult women needed to value ourselves.

As I observed women and how our choices can affect our lives and our children's lives as well as society at large; I am truly committed to sharing and helping young women value themselves.

I have shared some of these stories with my daughters in hopes that they never experience this treatment in their lives. I have made it very clear to all my sons-in-law that my husband and I will not tolerate any of our children being mistreated and disrespected on any level.

Women should be very careful selecting their mates if they are serious about selecting someone who will provide a healthy and functional life for them and their children.

We should take our time to talk to our prospective mates. Talk and observe their relationships with others. Don't ignore signs; signs that your prospect may have control issues; self-esteem issues, or "wandering eyes".

Be wary if they are disrespectful to you and your family; if they are distrustful or don't recognize when they are wrong and can't apologize.

Conversations and issues of abuse should be discussed before you commit. Make it clear that you will not tolerate any verbal or physical abuse in any form.

Often we don't mention to our partners that we will not tolerate mental or physical abuse; however, when it happens we accept a "fake apology" and continue.

Teach your partner how you want to be treated; this goes for both genders.

Pay attention to cultural differences because you may not get support from the women in that group when you need assistance. However, make sure you have a good support group around you to discuss important matters.

It is also important to not be an abuser yourself. It is not acceptable for a woman to abuse her husband; too often some women think it's cute to use the "tongue" to belittle the man and expect him to take the verbal abuse because they are not inflicting physical pain. Let's use our words to advise, comfort, suggest, correct, and forgive!

One day I was at work when I got the "call". On the other side of the phone was a nurse from a hospital calling to tell me that my mother was in the hospital and not doing well.

I left work and drove towards Queens Hospital where she was admitted. I didn't know why she was there because I spoke to her a few days earlier.

While driving down Belt Parkway, I received another call, this time from her doctor stating that he didn't think she would "make it". I began to pray that she would be alive until I got there to say a few words and say goodbye.

I prayed and prayed and thought of all the moments I lost as her daughter. The times and relationships my daughters would miss.

As I got off the elevator and walked down the hallway I felt I had only a few moments with her. As I entered the room doctors and nurses were standing by her bed. Her monitor was still beeping but not for long. I held her hand and stroked her hair.

She was leaving me as the tears rolled down my cheeks. I thanked her for being my mother. I thanked her for loving us in her way. As I closed my eyes as the beeping sound faded.

I told her it was O.K, I would be fine. As I closed my eyes I saw her in a beautiful white lace dress laying on a wooden raft slowly drifting on the ocean as if she was sleeping. She looked so peaceful.!

I don't know how long I was standing there but it must have been a while because the nurse said she was calling me several times and I was not responding until she shook me a little.

As the nurse looked at me, she said, "Your mom passed". I responded "I know, she is truly at peace, I saw her." I continued to stand by my mom's bedside while they wrapped her body, placed her on the stretcher, and removed all the machines she was hooked up to. I walked with the nurse towards the mortuary as the doors closed.

After my mother's passing, it took me some years before I would speak with my father. I continued to pray to God that I would forgive him one day.

For me to release my anger. I had certain conditions that would make me talk to him; one condition for me was that he apologize for his treatment of our mother; to admit he was a bad husband to his wife and at times a poor father to his children; that he greatly contributed to her mental illness or was at least a great participant in moving her in that direction. And that he caused her a lot of pain and didn't care about its consequences on his children.

I was not going to pretend that my mother's illness was all her fault. I was not going to pretend that she didn't matter. Because she mattered so much to me.

Over the years, I would find myself reading books on mental illness. Listening and watching shows that addressed the issues. I listened to some self-healing tapes that helped me take the first step toward mending my relationship with my father.

My husband helped a great deal in talking with me about rekindling my relationship with my father.

I decided one day I would pick up the phone and call him to say hello. Keeping the conversation brief; as the phone rang, I was nervous because I had not talked to him for over 20 years. He answered and I started the conversation with "Hi Dad, how are you? I am just checking in. How are you doing? Did you go for your walk today?" He asked me the same questions. I promised to check in more frequently. The conversation was brief, and I promised him I would call again. Our calls would be several weeks apart, sometimes months.

One weekend I decided to invite him over to our home for Sunday brunch; which I had every Sunday with my family as a ritual. He accepted the invitation, but I also invited my brothers because I was not ready to do "Kumbaya" with only him. It would be a long process for me to get there.

My husband was truly surprised and so were our daughters —some of whom were in high school. This was the first time my father met some of his grandchildren. I prayed that our meeting would be pleasant.

At this time in my life, I had become an exceptional woman. A woman that was not afraid to be me. I could tolerate being uncomfortable for a few hours.

My father was now in his 70s and hadn't enjoyed the benefits of his grandchildren. I asked God for guidance in approaching this new relationship.

I realized my father was a product of his culture as well. He did what was taught to him by example. Surprisingly, he didn't experience an abusive father, however, it was very prevalent in his culture. In some cultures, there was only one way men could show their manhood: To be very dominant, abusive, and controlling.

I realized that I could not change what was done. However, it was in my hands and God's will to live my life the way I would like it to be.

I decided to forgive my father despite him not meeting any of my 'conditions for forgiveness' and try to develop a relationship for both our sake. For me, I learned that you can't hold on to anger and disappointments in your life; because you end up suffering and others, like your children, miss out on a relationship with their extended families.

Our daughters grew up loving my husband's parents. They always asked about their grandfather, my father, and I couldn't explain to them at the time that I was having my issues. However, as my daughters were becoming young women I felt it was important to have this conversation. There was a lot more to the story other than just my father's abuse of my mother. Other family secrets had to be hidden for the sake of my children's innocence.

Our daughters have always seen a great example of what a father figure should be. The girls went everywhere with their father and he enjoyed their company. Whenever he went to the mosque to worship, the girls went with their 'daddy' to the mosque to pray. There, they made lifelong friends and became strong examples to their peers.

Their father changed their diapers from birth, feeding and comforting them. He woke them up during the night to use the bathroom to avoid bedwetting.

My husband took them to school and picked them up. He sat with them patiently and did homework and studies with them. One of the favorite meals that he made often was scrambled eggs; mine couldn't compare.

My husband and I were young parents and we took our roles and responsibilities seriously. Our lives revolved around our children. I decided early on in my youth that I would not choose a man like my father, and not allow any man to mistreat me. My rock was always God as my protector. I always asked for protection and guidance.

I have noticed that too many women trap themselves with men who are popular amongst women and those are typically the ones who can't sit still, they often continue seeking attention and approval from other women.

Throughout the years since reopening my relationship with my father; our daughters have been involved in his life. They have visited him and some have stayed overnight in his home.

My father always talks about them and he shows how proud he is of me. I smile on the inside to think that life has a way of teaching us all kinds of lessons.

I realized that I should not expect an apology from someone who maybe is in a lot of pain. You will have to forgive them for God's sake and not allow the behavior to be acceptable moving forward. Since my parents divorced he was in several relationships and fathered several children since; none of which I have met. This is too often the lives of many males.

I am convinced that men and women need to be prepared for marriage and that it is important to have an extended family as support. Although I came from a dysfunctional divorced family I didn't allow that experience to define what I would become.

Dad is now 90 and going strong. I often sit and talk to him about his life trying to get some insight; however, he seems to feel "safe" talking about politics; which is something we all like to do. He particularly likes to talk about Guyanese politics in Guyana. As time passes, I continue to get to know him; I realize that we have a few things in common; such as: exercising, walking (which we both do in the mornings whenever we can), eating healthy, and other positive lifestyle activities.

I realized that the way he expresses himself about life and relationships now, is probably how he wishes he was. He gives advice to my brothers and shows support to his grandchildren and gives encouragement to them. He is the proud grandfather of several grandchildren and many great-grandchildren.

My beloved mother Gloria is ever present in my heart and life. I truly believe that I am the woman I am today because of her and the fact that I paid attention to her life and learned through her lessons.

All the abuse I witnessed affected me — my heart, my mind, my soul, throughout my childhood into my adult years.

For me and all the children of domestic violence, divorce, and other painful experiences, we have choices in life. You can sit wondering why your life was not "perfect" like you wanted it to be or you can redefine your life to be productive and a blessing to others.

It's not easy moving forward but life is full of choices; have the power to choose in life whether you want to repeat negative behaviors or create your path of kindness, positivity, consciousness, and progress. Be prepared for the consequences of either choice.

You must constantly have standards for yourself; love yourself constantly. Take care of your mental and physical health. Have alone time; go to the spa, travel, volunteer to help others; share your experiences, however, still be guarded with your time and information.

Keep your Creator at the front of your life, always. People are often happy when events go in their favor but quick to give up on God when things don't go their way. You have to remember that the creator is ever-present. You should be having conversations every second of the day with the creator!

I can now call my father, my dad, and someone I can say I am learning to love and respect. I have let go of all the ill feelings towards him. My reflection on him now revolves around some of the most valuable lessons he taught me. Education was very important to my parents. My dad enforced it and my brothers and I made sure we took our education seriously. When I reflect on our lives as children, I thank God every day for his blessings. Our faith could have been weak; we could have gone down the wrong path. We were so vulnerable to everything. My brothers could have joined gangs or sold drugs; because all of it was available to us. I could have been promiscuous and gotten pregnant as a teenager. But, what I truly believed saved us was our belief that God would save us. I had many distractions that could have easily destroyed me. No one was caring for us but God.

I watched over my little brothers and allowed them to be little boys. They built

their little go-carts in the backyard and
sidewalks and had fun. They were very
respectful of their big sister. They came
into the house when playtime was over
and did their studies. I don't think that
they had a clue about most of the chaos
that was occurring around them. If they
did, they didn't express it much. All of my
brothers are exceptional fathers and I
could not be more proud.

You are either in tribulations or blessings.
I believe God helps those who truly help
themselves out of their conditions. You
must have faith that life will always get
better and put your actions toward that.
Always put in the work for good and you
will get positive results. Maybe not
immediately, but it will show up in
unexpected places and occurrences.

When life may seem unacceptable to you,
step up to the challenge and do it better

to make a difference. Always try to see the best in everyone and don't be ashamed of your past circumstances.

It will take some time to adjust to the hurt. However, remember you have choices. Often when others see you as being successful in life, the assumption is that you were always that way Not realizing that it was a process and continues to be so!!

Appreciate that you were born and these experiences that you had in the past will NOT define you in the future. We should all be aware that others' opinions of us should never define who we are.

My intention in writing this book is to be purposeful. I counseled for over a dozen years in public high schools to students from various cultures; who have shared horror stories in confidence with me; we were able to process our way through the "madness" and the pain. I was blessed to impact so many young lives.

Encourage yourself and others to be their best. Whatever their best is will be up to them. But, as human beings, we sometimes don't see our potential when others do. Be supportive of others and stop trying to be competitive. Be competitive with yourself and you will be fine. Support your children even when times get rough and they are not sure of themselves. Remember, we were once in their "shoes". Most of all, be supportive of those around you; and start with yourself.

A letter to Gloria

Dear Gloria,

How are you today? I hope this letter finds you in the best of spirits. I just wanted to say that I finally have learned to appreciate you as my mother. The lessons you have given me are so invaluable. I know now that when I was growing up as a little girl and a young woman I seemed lost, angry, and confused; you were too as well. I remember you saying to me "Why are you so angry, Madonna; you are so beautiful, everything will be fine".

Well, I never paid you any attention because you were the "crazy mother" I didn't want. Please forgive me for my ignorance and actions and attitude toward you. I didn't know any better, I was a child who was hurt and confused and was unable to express my emotions and thoughts.

You took me from a place as a child where my world was "perfect" with my grandparents and cousins to a place of uncertainty. Now, as an adult, I understand what you were going through. I can forgive you because you did what you thought was best.

In my reflection on my life with you, I am happy that you brought us to be with you and my dad. Maybe you knew how things (life) would turn out for us.

I love you mother and will always carry you with me. I am a better person; a caring human being because of you. I remember how kind you were to your parents and siblings. I wish I could have been as much of a loving, caring daughter and person as you. However, God had better things and more exciting adventures for you and that's alright with me. You were always a God-fearing woman who always wanted to do God's word and live a Godly life. I learned a lot from your presence and life. Although you may not have lived the life you deserved, your offspring have walked in your path. You would be proud. I told them of your story, as a loving daughter, sister, and mother. Thank you so much for being my mother!

Sincerely,
Madonna Ellis Knight

If you or someone you love are currently
facing domestic violence, please call the
National Domestic Violence Hotline for
assistance; 1800-799-7233

———

For speaking engagements and other
inquiries please email
madonna.knight@gmail.com

I REMEMBER GLORIA   MADONNA KNIGHT